Life's Ballet

Charles Schlee

Contents

the thank-you card

as you can see
it's very pretty
in its plain
and simple way

its thank-you
hardly gritty
speaks of kindness
how it lights one's day

and though the words
are not that witty
it matters
what they have to say

yet we so often lose their sense
which is a real pity
as we pirouette and leap
in life's ballet

the dialogue

in the darkness
suddenly i saw it

it went up
and then back down

it briefly paused
then up it went again

i tried to make it out
but couldn't seem to

there i stood
not knowing what to do

for me
this kind of dialogue
was
after all
quite new

not done
it then went back
where it had been

and stayed there
for a while

and as it looked at me

it almost seemed to smile

without warning
up it went again

then hovered for a while
till off it flew

and there i stood
with nothing but the shape
that in my heart
it drew

a wish

i've never met you
likely never will
but have a message
that i'd like to send you still

about the two of you
the things you do and say
directed at each other
as you walk along your way

it's clear you have deep feelings
for each other
but the passing years
so easily
our deepest joys can smother

i hope you will be happy
free from harm
and that your times together
will hold for you a certain charm

but winter cold will come
and you will wish you still could cling
to the gentle warmth
of spring

the cool air
warm sun
dew upon the grass

the freshness
we
to our relationships
forget at times
to bring

like when we listen to a voice
that isn't there
hearing but cacophony
suspended in the air

or see a form
whose movements are so brisk
they leave us feeling
it's no longer safe to take the risk

or sense a harshness
in a glance or tone
that
overlook it though we try
still chills us to the bone

and then
we pull away
afraid that
this relationship
leaves little room to stay

and yet
it needn't be like this

struggle
though

at times we may
life needn't be
an endless fray

so by the time each day is through
may each of you
have bathed the other
in the spring-like freshness
of the morning dew

the acorn

it rolled
and bounced
and hurried right along
like it was moving to the rhythm
of a song

it may have had
some place to go
it hurried so

or maybe
it had sat upon the ground
for so much time
it simply felt a need
to wander round

another curious notion
is that maybe it was
put in motion
by a twig
or squirrel
or the wind

or possibly
against some oaken deity
had sinned

in any case
there seemed no looking back

it must have thought it best
to take a different tack

and so it just kept moving
right along

too soon it took its leave
from the path that i was on

and left me
on my own
to face the moments
that i couldn't yet have known

a life apart[1]

with burning flesh
and burning heart
i'll spend my life
apart
until the embers
of my flesh and heart
at length
my life do part

you grew up in the court of a norman king
not drawn to courtly splendors
you would sink into your depths
to seek therein
the one you could not be separated from

when offered to a count in marriage
you sought refuge in a nunnery
yet finding little peace therein
you moved into a cave
to bring you closer to
the one you could not be separated from

you grew in strength and courage
till
one day
you knew you had to look
once more
upon the world from which you'd come
to quench what fleshly embers burned within

and so you found a cave
from which to view the world of your youth
and there you stayed
till
in your dying breath
you were
at length
transported to
the one you could not be separated from

with burning flesh
and burning heart
i'll spend my life
apart
until the embers
of my flesh and heart
at length
my life do part

the legacy of now

though we'd thought about it often
we had doubts about
the distance
and the cost
but finally we chose to do it
anyway

it was a long
and tiring
drive

we drove through
prairies
foothills
mountains
deserts
far from our accustomed view

despite the curves
and traffic
and the random speeding cars
we never felt
in harm's way

we passed trucks
that seemed to caravan along the highways
and saw trains
that seemed to stretch for miles

we drove through reservations
and saw houses in the distance
sitting at the bottoms of the hills
near dusty roads

at length
we reached
where we had hoped to be
with an agenda full
of sights and sounds
and stories we would tell
on our return

yet what
in all of this
would we
discern

and how

what would be the legacy
of now

the mother

she sat there
quite content

when asked
she wanted to consent
and so she did
nothing here to resent

it was to her
a marvelous event
so she accepted
with the best intent

perhaps
this is a fable
but they say
she birthed him in a stable
and then raised him
the best that she was able

later when she saw
how they would him torment
she felt a pang
but even then did not lament

some say she mothered god
others
not so fast
in any case

hers is a story
that will last

although for her this was
a steep ascent
never was she
spent

as through her life
she went
living
her consent

they say that she
was taken up
to join her son
when her life's work
was done

her many challenges
she never tried to circumvent
in her devotion
never bent

hers was a role
that
surely
had been heaven-sent

it's french

to loosen
and to tighten
so that things will fit together
is the common purpose
of a wrench

but our focus here
is french

a language many people speak
perhaps because they need to
or perhaps because they like
its nasal hue

and yet
this language
can be challenging

sometimes it's hard to make it out
they talk so fast
as if for fear that what they say
might be in concrete cast
but you can't fix that with a wrench
it's french

they try to keep their language pure
with their académie française
as if a lack of purity
would cause malaise

but you can't fix that with a wrench
it's french

at times a final consonant liaises
while at others not
it's quite a phonologic mess
they've got
but you can't fix that with a wrench
it's french

before an h there's liaison
except when h is aspiré
if this gets any more complex
i'd best be on my way
but you can't fix that with a wrench
it's french

with origins in vulgar latin
and an added gaulish flavor
it's evolved into a language
many savor

it has many oddities
that have become quite set
yet if we fixed it
who knows what we'd get

and if we tightened it
too much
we'd lose its sound and flow
and such

so even if we could
why fix it with a wrench
why not accept the simple fact
it's french

going

some say
that all roads lead to rome
but what if rome
is not our home

might it not be better
then
to roam

at least that way
we stand a chance
to find a place to stay

as we so often think
we need to do

but is this true

what if our place
is out in space
or in the very depths of matter

in a look
or way to cook

or in a kind of touch
that we don't get
that much

or in our chatter
or the ways we
our opinions
scatter

many are the places
we can stay

and we so often
think
there is a space
that is
our special place

as if the reason
why we roam
is but to
find a place
we're able to call home

yet any space
can disappear
however far
or near

and when it does
we feel
we have no choice
except to listen
to another voice

so on we wander
down a different path

that
be it short
or long
we trust
will make us strong

till one day
tired of the memories
of places left behind
and of the anguished longing
for the many
that we yet might find

we fix our gaze
on what we've done

and see that
what had drawn us
all along
was but the going

not the gone

a monk's freedom[2]

he was kneeling in his room
pondering the life he'd chosen
and the many lives he'd given up
when
suddenly
he realized
how often
he'd said no

to wealth
to fame
to pleasure
to the kind of joy
that comes from feeling
others care

and somehow
he got stuck
on all
the times
and ways
his life had flowed from
no

without that no
how different he'd have been
not sitting now
a recluse
in his room

communing
with his god
but lost
instead
in matters of the world

disciplined and humble
still he couldn't help but smile
as he pondered
his relentless no
how much he'd chosen
not to do
or say
or feel

he'd framed a way of life
built on a simple
no

and now
for him
the world around him
in a sense
existed
only as
what he had mastered
with a no

and yet
since he'd not made it come to be
it was a world
that
given its immenseness

surely must have been created
by his god

a god
who could have made it
any way he pleased

and then the monk
reflected on
the nature of his god

on what his god must be
to have created
all the things that one can see

to be so free

the monk acknowledged
that he didn't know
what god began with
maybe remnants of a former world
or maybe
when he started
there was nothing there at all

and then there crossed the mind
of this reclusive monk
a thought
he'd never wrestled with
before

what if the world had flowed
from an idea
in god's mind

if so
what other thoughts
what other worlds
might there have been
to which god had said
no

kneeling in his room
before a cross
and feeling closer now
than ever
to his god
the monk felt heartened
by this sudden revelation

as he brought his meditation
to a close
he thanked his god
for helping him to see
a deeper manner
in which he is free

and how
so very like his god
is he

the doing

i see her cross the street
ahead of me
and as we pass
we smile
and wave

i've seen her walk to school
many times
in the early morning hours
and i look forward to this chance
to greet her

she seems friendly
someone i would like
to get to know
though likely
never will

i don't know
what she does in school
what grades she gets
or how she lives her life
outside that moment
when we pass

i only know
her gentle wave
and smile

her doing
for a momentary
while

and though
once we have passed
the doing is
in its way
done
it doesn't have to birth a daughter
or a son

its sparkle's
in the doing

not the done

giving thanks

i guess
we ate some turkey
though my recollection's
kind of murky

she had fixed
a lot of sides
each one of which
of course i tried

as usual
i'd overeaten
as if soon
my maker i'd be meetin'

and for me
it was a restful day
though not a place in which
i'd want for long to stay

yet i suppose that giving thanks
is good
and that from time to time
we should

for after all
if we our thanks be givin'
then at least
we still be livin'

singularly me[3]

i died
read my obituary
written by my brother

surely he's
a fitting author
being
as he's been for years
the family genealogist
hence able
my accomplishments
to list

and so
of course
i read it

after all
it's me

or is it

it summarizes
many of the things i did
and gives a nice synopsis
of a life

but is that
what i was

in a sense
i guess so
after all
i did the things he wrote about

but surely there was more to me
than just the things i did

for wasn't i the doer
of the did

had it been done
by someone else
it wouldn't have been
me

i guess
what makes it me
isn't just
that it was done
but its uncompromising singularity
as something
that was done by me

so in a sense
i'm what i did
i'm all the things
a genealogist can say

but i am also
something more
that no one else can be

for though another
might have done it
it was i
and i alone
who lived
the doing of the did

a living
that
no matter how you look
and what you see
was
irrefutably
uncompromisingly
and
singularly
me

the jump[4]

prizing your virginity
your heart took shelter
far from worldly pursuits

not sharing your convictions
those in power thought it fit
to still the faith within you

so
one day
when you were just fifteen
some soldiers came to fetch you

knowing the abuse that you would face
you asked the soldiers
if they'd let you change your clothes

when they agreed
you left the room
ran to the roof

and jumped

your lifeless body
now lay cradled by the sea

some folks will ask
why did you jump
and by what right

for after all
there's not just what we do
there's what we might

yet each of us
is guided by our sight
and
like a tender seedling
sprouting in the night
must keep on reaching upward
toward the light

his despair

he didn't have a lot
made do with what he got
but when he asked himself
if he was satisfied
he knew that he was not

it wasn't that he wanted more
or just got lost
in others' lore

he simply needed
somewhere else to go
in order
other seed to sow

when seeking insight
he felt free
had always been intrigued
by how to be

they say
it's who you know
not what
that spells success
as on life's path you go

yet he
the who that really mattered

never knew
the things that others saw

they simply
didn't fall
within his view

he looked for insights
everywhere he went
his drive to understand
was never spent

he slowly came to see
that others
had a different way to be

a way
he never could embrace
for fear
he would himself debase

though never claiming to be wise
perhaps he was too meek
yet
as he went through life
he couldn't help but seek
whatever beckoned out there
even though
he never could say what
or where

he
as we all do

wanted those around
to see the things that he saw
too

yet no one ever seemed to look
and so he put his thoughts
into a book
in the hope that others
might it read
and realize
that they too
shared his need

but no one
ever read his book
or even seemed to care
to take a look

he'd always thought
that others
the same insights
surely sought

but though his insights
shone for him
as he was guided by their lustre
others seemed to act
on whim

and as for insights
one would give one's life for
others always seemed to wish for less
not more

so as the years burnt on
and left their smoke
the prize
was never won

his hope
now crumbling into bits
he felt as someone falling
through an endless pit

and with his life
fast coming to its end
he knew that
down his chosen path of insight
soon
he would no longer wend

then
suddenly
it came to him
that there was something
he no longer could forbear

a final insight
to which
surely
he was heir

how to live out
his despair

i know not what i do[5]

i joined them
for a brief foray
into their inner worlds

could not embrace them
couldn't grace them
did not know how to stay

as they spoke of god the father
i longed for god
the mother

as they looked for mercy from without
i craved but mercy
from within

as they stood to state their faith
i could only stand
and wait

as they gave up all resistance
i could only share
my distance

and so i put them down
not wanting
them around

and looked at them as somehow less
not truly whole
not blessed

then as they left
i reached within myself
and felt a gentle longing

and as i felt it
so i sensed
that those whom i had faulted
were following
like me
but what to them
seemed heaven-sent

and then i felt
a sense of shame
at faulting those
whose only sin it was
to stay somewhere
beyond my willing ken

perhaps forgiveness is too late
yet now i have a place
for them
and for their longings too
for i share with them their fate

i know not what i do

the scavenger

there it was
on the floor

i saw it just in time
to step aside

luckily i noticed
though it barely moved
and looked much like
a speck of dirt

i then continued
with my sweeping
and my scooping

cats
though good at grooming
don't their messes
clean

what would have happened
to that little bug
had i not seen it
when i did

it might have changed its habitat
from floor to sack
with gobs of moistened litter
to explore

it might have found
a residence
in insect heaven

let us hope

or might have fallen
from the dustpan
just in time

there may
of course
be other explanations

these are merely those
that come to mind

in any case
it would have lived
an altered life

or
maybe
none at all

i suppose
it didn't see me coming
though i'd done so
many times

perhaps i was so big
it simply didn't notice

maybe it was taken
by a movement even smaller
on the floor

yet it
despite my looming presence
whether by sheer luck
my lack of inattention
even my agility
simply kept on being
what it was

a scavenger of basement floors

a meditation[6]

he took it
from the table
by his bed

and opened it
of course

after all
it was
his trusted source

he longed to read it
yet again
perhaps
his gravest sin

yet who would want
to walk in darkness
when a light
was near at hand

and why not learn
to love and serve his god
who'd surely
in agreement
nod

and anyway
it was the only life he knew

a life he cherished
being
as he surely was
among the chosen few

so once again
he'd fill his mind
with how to be
a humble servant
of his god

he didn't seek
to know about the world
or understand the movements
of the skies

he simply didn't seek to know

to him
the only thing that mattered
was a humble life of service

so to get the insights
that he sought
he read
and read
and read
longer
than he'd ever read
before

eventually he tired

but when he set the book
back on the table
by his bed
his thoughts
began to float away

at first a few
then many more
until his mind
was empty

and at peace

and then
it came to him

he had been striving
every day
to find out
how to serve his god
and live a humble life

he'd tried
each day
to quell the doubts
that lingered
once he closed the book
and left it
on the table
by his bed

and yet
by striving thus to know

he'd built a wall
that hid from view
the presence
he so deeply
and so long
had sought

he'd finally let go
and felt an openness
he could not now ignore

he knew
his less
was more

to whom i talk

i've spoken to you
many times
in many forms
and rhymes

i've heard your voices
speak to me
in prose
as well as poetry

i know that you
a friend could be
if only you would
talk to me

but
in the end
i hear but monologue
from which you never bend

i trust you see the pertinence
of what i say
and of the feelings
i display

and though my manner
is direct
despite my words
i mean no disrespect

i merely wish
that you
would say
a word or two

and though you live
but in your books
in which alone still shine
your special looks

i cannot help but wonder
as i grieve
if you might give
a brief reprieve

walking her dog

i'd made the turn
around the fountain
and had just begun
my walk back home

and then i glimpsed her
walking briskly
with her dog
across the street

and heard her
as i often had before
loudly and austerely
talking to her dog

approaching now the crosswalk
which i'd seen her cross before
i knew she'd likely cross
to my side of the street

and since she always walked
so briskly
knew she'd pass me
soon

i walked along
when suddenly
i heard a bark
and glimpsed a leaping form

i turned and saw her dog
attempting
so it seemed
to greet me

but she brusquely muttered something
to her dog
and kept her gaze
fixed straight ahead

i'd hoped
that this might be
a chance to smile
and say hello

but there would be no smile
and no hello
for suddenly she ran
till she was well ahead of me

once she'd resumed a walking gait
she turned
looked briefly back
then crossed the street again

now on the other side
she turned around and looked at me
as if she needed to confirm
that i was staying put

she then walked briskly on

a tale of two fissures[7]

in the beginning
there was being
a fullness
content within itself

then
one day
a fissure developed

no one knows why
or how

it just happened

a little bit of nothingness
had entered into being

being was now *for* itself
and could get a little distance from itself
while still remaining present to itself

this fissure
this nothingness within being
was able not just to *be*
but to give birth to *possibilities*
and to pursue these possibilities
and feel
in many ways
filled as it did so

but it could never get enough of that feeling
for no sooner did it feel it had finally been filled
than the feeling disappeared
and it again was empty
condemned to pursue yet another possibility
on what seemed an endless path

it quickly discovered
it was not alone

as it strained to reach its possibilities
it felt looked at
skewered to its very depths
by other fissures it encountered on its way

and thus it lived
always for
never with

then
one day
it disappeared

some say it clashed with another fissure
others say it just gave up
but the fissure was no more

it could no longer dream of possibilities and their pursuit
nor enjoy the fullness that provided

it lived only in the memories and dreams
of other fissures

one day
another fissure formed
but this one was different

like all fissures
it too was but a crack in being
a something that was
well
nothing

but
unlike the fissures around it
it did not long to be filled
in fact
it enjoyed its emptiness
sometimes it would spend hours lost in it
then seemingly
without notice
surge forth
and once again do all the sorts of things that fissures do

being could
finally
be *with* itself

this fissure
too
felt looked at
by other fissures

yet it never lost its sense of nothingness
why would it
after all

it *was* nothingness
and that was fine

it never clashed with other fissures
or at least it never tried to
even when they picked a fight
it wasn't interested in winning

it encouraged other fissures
to delve into their own depths too
although they always seemed afraid
of being swallowed up by
nothing

thus it lived

always with
never for

then one day
it too
disappeared

though most of the fissures
seemed oblivious to its absence
one went off by itself
and sat for days
thinking
and wondering
then
finally
took a chance

and delved into the depths
of its nothingness

and thus
the fissure
that had disappeared
lived on

undaunted[8]

not just ideas
to be bantered
bartered
borne
your faith infused you
heartened every filament thereof
until your faith and life
became as one

yet they
complying with their duty
tried to douse what fire burned within
to lure you with the endless promise of your youth
if only you'd recant

but you trod forth
undaunted

so they placed you on a rack
and tore your youthful flesh
with iron hooks
and when their work was done
to show you mercy
or perhaps just tired of your gaze
lopped off your head

it may be out of weakness
or just curiosity

that now i ask
what was the point of all your torment

after all
you could have walked away

if you had but renounced your faith
you would have lived
to see another day

yet those who differed
held no sway
as you
before them
lay

sisters

many of us have them
which need not be bad
although at times
they make us feel sad

some of us have sisters
that we like
whom even in our dreams
we'd never strike

some of us have sisters
that we tolerate
in spite of all the ways they find
to irritate

some of us have sisters
that can leave us not quite whole
the kind that gives us blisters
on our souls

regardless of the sisters
we have known or had
and whether they have
made us mad or glad

the conduct of a sister
who won't see beyond her ways
can hit you like a twister
on a summer day

talking

you say that i don't talk that much
about the two of us
and what we want to do
and such

and yet
we spend much of our time
together
in a kind of living rhyme

we see each other often
and we like the things we see
the things that make us
you and me

what then are the things
we're in such need of finding out
the things
we really need to talk about

we share a little
of our lore
but through our touches
so much more

what matters in the end
seems less the distance of our talk
than that our times together
yield a strong yet tender stalk

walking along[9]

i heard the traffic
on the highway
which i hear
near every day
as i take
my morning walk
and to myself
i talk

and i don't hold this pesky virus
in disdain
nor those who are infected
in the main
i simply hope
that it will stay
at least six feet
away

i pass the park
and see
a man and dog
a friendly way to be
they're coming toward me now
on their side
of a bike path
that is happily quite wide

we say hello
and pass

it's not the first time
nor i trust the last

enjoying the cool air
i walk along
then hear a voice
is it a song
or just
some friendly chatter
that
to her now seems to matter

we say hi
and wave
at least we're not yet
in the grave

then suddenly i glimpse a woman
coming toward me
with her dog
and my brief chance i see
to say hello
which she then follows with a nod
as she says something sternly
to her dog
both walking briskly on in their accustomed way

i pass the fountain
with its orange tulips
battered by a recent rain
and
glad to be alive
i turn to go back home

the german in me

i try the things he says
to understand

his words paint simple pictures in the mind
as if we six or seven years of age were

yet i fail to understand
why he in this way speaks

i've heard that he of german lineage is
though he instead a swedish ancestry once claimed

rejecting thus one's birthright
makes to me no sense

i like the german language and its grammar's ins and outs
it helps my thoughts to clarify

i am to german deeply drawn
in spite of struggling in my native tongue to live

i know not
whether this an illness be

but i would such an illness long endure
in order not from what i am to run

though i in germlish spoke

the storm[10]

the clouds are dark
there's lightening in the distance
thunder too

he likes to go on walks
and though a storm approaches
does what he is prone to do

and so he walks

why not
he's walked in storms before
many times in fact

why
would he now
take a different tack

and so he walks

the wind grows stronger
as it often does
before a storm

yet he doesn't mind
the wind and rumbles
in the early hours of the morn

and so he walks

he feels some drops
then many more
as it begins to rain

but it is only water
and to him
it doesn't matter in the main

and so he walks

as he feels the gusts of wind
he has to hold his cap
lest it should blow away

and though his clothes are getting soaked
in the rain
is where he'll surely stay

and so he walks

the wind grows stronger
the rain gets harder
water rushes down the edges of the streets

yet to him
to walk in wind and rain
is but another feat

and so he walks

and i suppose that
if you ask him
why he walks on rainy morns

he'll say
why not
for what's the point of walking
if you won't do it in a storm

life's ballet

many are the trappings
of the lives we lead

we focus on the things
we think we need
until one day
we find them bent
or rent
or simply spent

and yet
how hard it is
to give up
what we've worked so hard to be

so then we fight
as best we can
to set things right

and often
by the movements that we make
and by the pain
we scatter in their wake

we miss
the most important thing
that we
to our relationships
can bring

for though our strength
is partly in our wit
it's mostly
in our fit

not in the bumps
that raise a fuss
but in the leaps
and pirouettes
that make
of you and me
an us

Notes

[1] This poem is about Saint Rosalia, a saint of the Roman Catholic Church. Little is known about her life. A brief biography may be found in https://catholicsaints.info/catholic-encyclopedia-saint-rosalia. Sicilian legends regarding Saint Rosalia have been incorporated into a 2013 post of the history blog of https://siciliangodmother.com

[2] This poem was inspired by "La liberté cartésienne." In Jean-Paul Sartre, *Situations philosophiques* (Paris: Éditions Gallimard, 1990), pp. 61-79.

[3] This poem was inspired by "L'universel singulier." In Jean-Paul Sartre, *Situations philosophiques* (Paris: Éditions Gallimard, 1990), pp. 295-325.

[4] This poem is about Saint Pelagia the Virgin, of whom a brief biography appears in https://en.wikisource.org/wiki/Catholic_Encyclopedia_(1913)/Pelagia.

[5] This poem is reprinted from Charles Schlee, *You Come Too* (www.xlibris.com : Xlibris, 2006, rev. 2019), pp. 35-36.

[6] This poem is inspired by the opening chapters of Thomas à Kempis, *The Imitation of Christ* (New York: Doubleday & Company, Inc., 1955).

[7] This poem is based on Jean-Paul Sartre's existential philosophy (as presented in *Being and Nothingness*) and my response (as presented in *An Anguished Crack in Being*).

[8] This poem is based on the life of Saint Epipodius, a saint of the Roman Catholic Church who lived in Lyon, France, during the second century. Information about him may be found in https://

catholicsaints.info/butlers-lives-of-the-saints-saints-epipodius-and-alexander-martyrs-at-lyons/.

9   This poem was written during the early months of the COVID-19 pandemic.

10   This poem is reprinted from Charles Schlee, *Random Lore* (www.xlibris.com : Xlibris, 2019), pp. 54-56.

www.ingramcontent.com/pod-product-compliance
Lightning Source LLC
Chambersburg PA
CBHW072038150726

47999CB00002B/967

* 9 7 8 9 3 8 8 3 1 9 1 6 4 *